Mysterious Journey

AMELIA EARHART'S LAST FLIGHT

ODYSSEY

Copyright © 1997 Trudy Corporation, 353 Main Avenue, Norwalk, CT 06851,
and the Smithsonian Institution, Washington, DC 20560

Soundprints is a division of Trudy Corporation, Norwalk, Connecticut.

Book design: Alleycat Design Inc. New York, NY

First Edition 1997
10 9 8 7 6 5 4 3 2 1
Printed in Hong Kong

Library of Congress Cataloging-in-Publication Data

Wickham, Martha, 1963–
        Mysterious journey : Amelia Earhart's last flight / by Martha Wickham : illustrated by
David Lund.
            p.   cm.
        Summary: While visiting the Amelia Earhart exhibit at the National Air and Space
Museum, Lucy travels back in time and becomes the famous pilot in the cockpit
of her last flight.
        ISBN 1-56899-407-9 (hardcover), -- ISBN 1-56899-408-7 (softcover)
        1. Earhart, Amelia, 1897–1937--Juvenile fiction. [1. Earhart, Amelia, 1897–1937--
Fiction. 2. Air pilots--Fiction. 3.Time travel--Fiction. 4. National Air and Space Museum--
Fiction.]
I. Lund, David, 1945– ill. II. Title.
PZ7.W6275My   1997
[E]--dc21   97-7244
                                                                                                        CIP
                                                                                                         AC

Mysterious Journey

AMELIA EARHART'S LAST FLIGHT

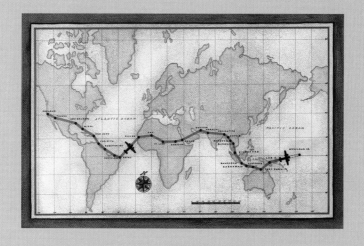

Written by Martha Wickham
Illustrated by David Lund

Soundprints
Where Children Discover...

"Look at that beautiful red plane," Lucy says with
a sigh. Lucy and her friends Emma, Kevin, and Tomas
are in the Amelia Earhart exhibit at the National Air
and Space Museum of the Smithsonian Institution.

"It's awesome!" Tomas says, staring at the Lockheed
Vega on display. "It says here that Amelia Earhart was
the first woman to make a nonstop solo flight across the
Atlantic Ocean."

"That's right," agrees Lucy. "She's the reason why
I joined the Young Eagles Program. Two pilots at the
airport in College Park have taken me flying with them
already. And I play a game called Flight Simulator on
my computer all the time."

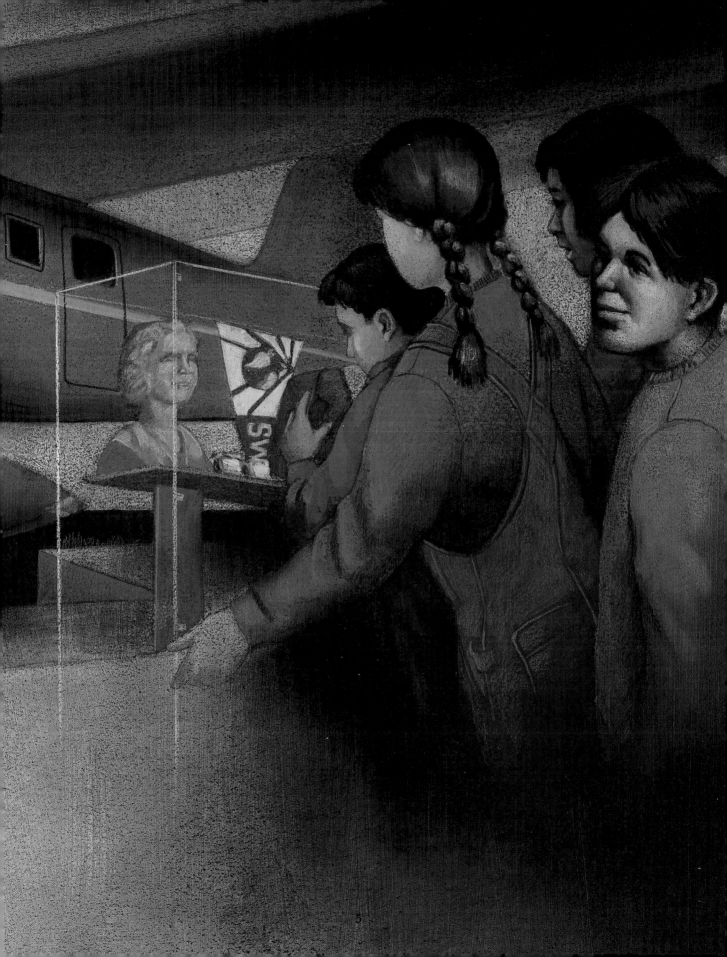

"Listen to this," Emma calls to the others. "Amelia disappeared while trying to fly around the world."

"She sent a message at 3:45 on the morning of July 3, 1937. Her message said, 'We are circling,'" Lucy recites from memory.

"She must have thought that she had found Howland Island, her next stop," Kevin says.

"Five hours later," continues Lucy, "Amelia radioed that she was flying back and forth, still looking for the island. It was at that moment that Amelia Earhart, her navigator Fred Noonan, and the Electra disappeared without a trace!"

Lucy gazes up at the black-and-white picture of Amelia, who is wearing pants tucked into high leather boots and a leather bomber jacket. "Boy, what I would give to have been able to meet Amelia Earhart."

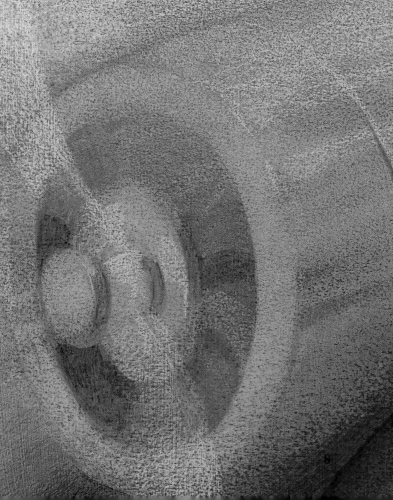

Asudden loud rumbling noise startles Lucy and causes her hands to shake! The noise is so overwhelming that it takes a moment for her to realize that she's not in the Amelia Earhart exhibit any longer. Instead, her hands are at the controls of an old-fashioned airplane and the plane is rumbling down a bumpy runway.

Lucy takes her eyes off the runway for a moment to notice that she's in a two-seater. There is a man sitting next to her. *He must be the navigator,* Lucy thinks.

The man says, "Ready for the next leg?"

Lucy looks back at the runway. The plane is reaching the end of the runway, and she has to do something fast. In front of her are nothing but choppy ocean waves. She realizes that a safe takeoff is completely up to her!

Lucy tries to remember the takeoffs in the Young Eagles Program as well as her hours of Flight Simulator. She pulls up on the yoke gently. With only 1,000 yards of runway, the cliff is getting closer and closer, and the ocean below looks bigger and more threatening all the time.

Suddenly they are in the air! The plane runs over the cliff and drops toward the water below. Just when she is sure the plane will end up in the ocean and they'll both drown, the nose lifts. They are airborne at last. Another five or six feet and they would have been trying to swim for shore!

The plane is heading up toward the blue sky. Far below, the ocean waves seem to dance. They are not frightening from up here!

This is fantastic, Lucy thinks. *It's no wonder Amelia Earhart loved to fly.*

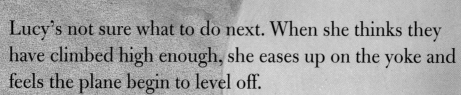

Lucy's not sure what to do next. When she thinks they have climbed high enough, she eases up on the yoke and feels the plane begin to level off.

Wow! she thinks to herself. I wish *Emma, Kevin, and Tomas were here with me now.*

Lucy still is not sure where she is, but she is excited and ready for adventure. She can hear the wind whistling against the sides of the plane. This is the thrill she loves most about flying.

"Good job, Amelia. You're one of the only pilots in the world who could have made that takeoff. Of course, I never had any doubts. You're a pro and the Electra is a good little plane."

Lucy is startled by the man's voice. She had almost forgotten that he was next to her. She turns to meet his smile and notices that his flight jacket has the name Noonan embroidered on the front.

"Thanks, Fred," Lucy answers. "That was exciting. I'm looking forward to this leg of the trip."

"Yes," Fred says. "I just hope this good weather will hold."

If I'm Amelia, Lucy thinks, *and he's Fred Noonan, then we must be on Amelia's last flight around the world. The flight where she disappeared over the Pacific Ocean and was never found.*

Yikes! Lucy thinks to herself. *I managed that takeoff okay, but what will happen next? What will happen to us?*

Although she's frightened, she manages a smile and says, "We'll be fine, Fred. We've gotten this far. We'll make it all the way."

"I'm not concerned, Amelia. That was a tough runway, though!" Noonan answers.

As she glances at the controls, Lucy realizes that, although this is a real plane, its control panel is very similar to Flight Simulator. There is an airspeed indicator, an altimeter, and a gas gauge.

Noonan's voice interrupts her thoughts. "I'm going to head back to the navigational table, Amelia."

"Right, Fred," Lucy answers.

"If you need me, just send a note back on the line," Noonan adds before getting out of the cockpit and back into the body of the plane.

At first Lucy cannot imagine what Fred is talking about. Then she notices a pulley mounted in the cockpit. Fishing line winds from the pulley and disappears behind her.

Lucy takes a quick peek over her shoulder and sees that the line ends at a pulley mounted on Noonan's navigational table. She sees a supply of pencils and paper beside both pulleys. She realizes that if she needs her navigator during the flight, she is to send a message back to him via the fishing line pulley system. *Pretty clever,* she thinks to herself.

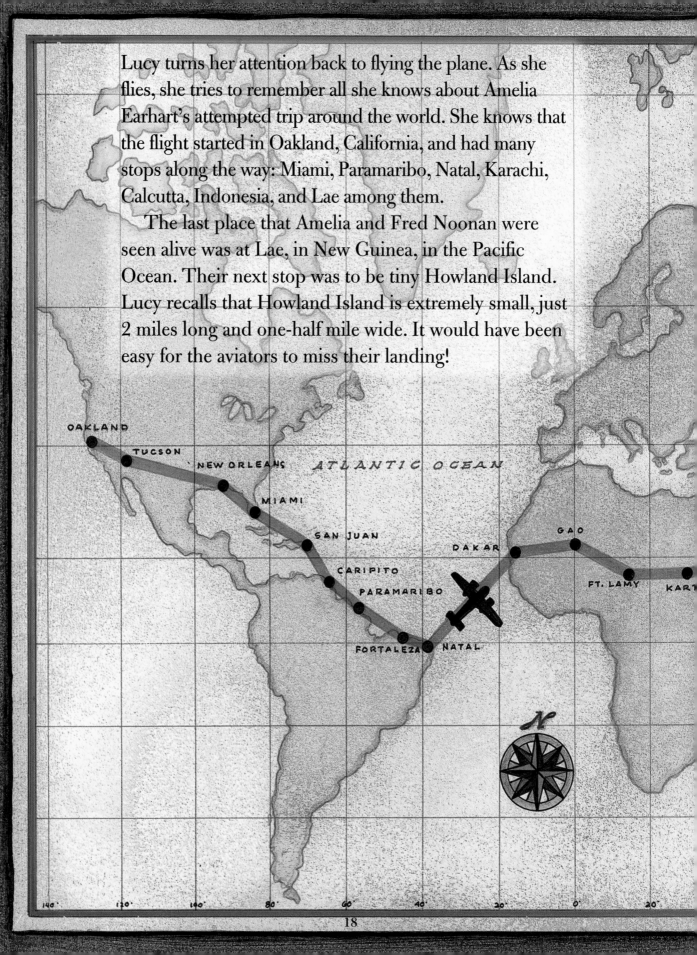

Lucy turns her attention back to flying the plane. As she flies, she tries to remember all she knows about Amelia Earhart's attempted trip around the world. She knows that the flight started in Oakland, California, and had many stops along the way: Miami, Paramaribo, Natal, Karachi, Calcutta, Indonesia, and Lae among them.

The last place that Amelia and Fred Noonan were seen alive was at Lae, in New Guinea, in the Pacific Ocean. Their next stop was to be tiny Howland Island. Lucy recalls that Howland Island is extremely small, just 2 miles long and one-half mile wide. It would have been easy for the aviators to miss their landing!

Grabbing a pencil stub and piece of paper, Lucy scribbles a quick note asking her navigator for the flight chart. She attaches it with a clip to the fishing line, and sends it back to Noonan. *This is like hanging clothes on a clothesline!* she thinks to herself. A moment later, the fishing line gently shakes, and then the chart appears.

Lucy unclips the chart and spreads it out on her lap. Shown clearly on this map of their journey are the island of New Guinea and the smaller islands in this section of the Pacific. There is a solid line drawn to Lae from a previous stop. There is just a dotted line connecting Lae to Howland Island.

With a gasp, Lucy realizes that they must be on the leg of the trip where Amelia's plane disappeared all those years ago—somewhere over the Pacific Ocean between Lae and Howland Island. Lucy might actually find out the truth about what happened to her hero!

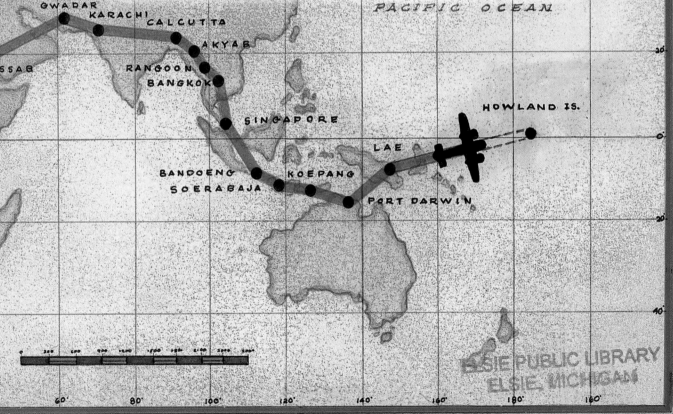

The pulley next to her begins to spin, and soon a note appears from Noonan:

Amelia, I've poured some hot cocoa. Can I get you anything? I know that we have raisins and chocolate, but I'm not sure what else.

The thought of food makes her stomach begin to churn. Lucy is surprised because she's never had problems when she's flown. Then she remembers that Amelia Earhart suffered from nausea!

No thanks, Fred. But thanks for sending up the chart. I'll transmit back to Lae now and let them know where we are.

Lucy tinkers with the clunky-looking radio on the floor next to her. When she's established contact, she announces that they are flying at 7,000 feet, are 800 miles east of Lae, and are right on course.

With the transmission complete, Noonan sends another note:

Only ten hours to go, Amelia. Keep up the good work!

Lucy smiles to herself, and continues to enjoy her flight.

Lucy admires the view around her while the sun begins to set. As the sky grows dark, she sees the most beautiful sunset she's ever seen.

The plane continues its comforting hum, making Lucy feel very calm and peaceful. The moon and stars begin to appear in the sky above.

As the sun slips below the horizon, Lucy notices that clouds are beginning to appear. Lucy knows that clouds can cause turbulence, which can make the plane buck and rock. She realizes that the nighttime flight might not be as smooth as the daytime flight has been. The responsibility of maintaining a safe and successful flight begins to weigh on her.

Grasping the radio microphone again, she requests a weather update from her team on Lae. She listens for a reply, but hears only static. Lucy tries several more times but is frustrated by the static she hears in response. Desperate as more clouds roll in, she sends another report back to Lae. This time she says, through heavy interference, "Cloudy…weather cloudy."

Lucy settles back into her seat. She hopes she's ready for whatever the night holds.

Lucy's fears about the weather are soon confirmed. A short time later, the Electra flies into heavier clouds. The plane begins to bump along. Lucy wonders if Amelia Earhart ever got nervous when her plane hit bad storms.

"Looks like we're headed right into a thunderstorm." Noonan says as he takes his place in the seat next to her.

"Yes," agrees Lucy. "I'll try to keep this as smooth as I can."

"I'm not worried," answers Noonan. "You've gotten us out of worse storms than this before."

Lucy is touched by Noonan's confidence. She will try to remember everything she knows about flying, but this is a big storm. Huge commercial jetliners, cruising at 30,000 feet, can usually fly above storms. In the Lockheed Electra, Lucy knows she doesn't have that choice. She's at 7,000 feet and there is nothing to do but continue to fly through the clouds.

She remembers what Amelia once wrote in a letter to her husband: "Please know that I am quite aware of the hazards. . . . Women must try to do things that men have tried. When they fail, their failure must be but a challenge to others."

As Lucy fights to keep the bucking plane on course, she thinks of the courageous Amelia Earhart, and it gives her renewed strength.

Suddenly, the plane flies out of a thick cloud into a pocket of clear night sky. Lucy sees another huge cloud ahead. Without a moment to spare, she grabs the radio mike. She knows she has only a short time to try to make contact.

She hears nothing but static. She keeps trying to transmit. Frustrated, Lucy begins to scream into the microphone, "Give me the weather! I've got to know the weather!" She listens for an answer. Nothing comes across except bursts of static. She repeats her request, but she's not sure if anything is coming through to Lae.

Lucy knows she has no choice; she must continue her flight.

Hoping she may still find out what really happened to her hero, Lucy flies on into the next cloud. Just ahead, a bolt of lightning snakes through the sky. It is followed by a thunderous boom.

For a split second, as the thunder claps, Lucy blinks her eyes.

When she opens them, she is startled to find herself standing next to the model of the Electra in the museum exhibit. She blinks again, then hurries over to a window. She hears another clap of thunder, and sees a large bolt of lightning. Lucy realizes that there is a storm brewing in Washington, D.C.

One minute she was thousands of feet above the Pacific Ocean, seeming to retrace Amelia Earhart's last flight. The next minute, she is back at the Smithsonian, admiring the Earhart exhibit. Lucy can still feel her hands shake from holding the controls of the plane so tightly.

"Hey, Lucy, ready to leave?" Tomas asks, joining her at the window.

"No way," Lucy answers. "I want to keep looking around."

The two join Emma and Kevin in the exhibit.

"It says here," Kevin reads, "that the U.S. Navy immediately began a huge search for the Electra, but they found nothing."

"You know," Emma says, "there is a rumor that some people think Amelia Earhart was captured by the Japanese."

"I think her plane just crashed into the ocean," says Tomas.

"I wonder if we'll ever know what happened," says Lucy. "But the one thing that we do know is that Amelia Earhart was a pioneer, and she was an inspiration to everyone."

Wherever you are, Amelia, Lucy thinks, *thanks for the adventure!*

About Amelia Earhart

Amelia Mary Earhart was born on July 24, 1897, in Atchison, Kansas. Always a daring and adventurous child, she was eleven when she saw a plane for the first time, at the Iowa State Fair. In 1920, after attending an airshow in Los Angeles, Amelia began flying lessons.

Soon she began setting records. In October 1922, she set the women's altitude record of 14,000 feet. In June 1928, she became the first woman ever to cross the Atlantic in a plane. In April 1931, she became the first woman to fly an autogiro (similar to a helicopter) across the United States. In January 1935 she was the first person to fly from Honolulu, Hawaii to Oakland, California.

The mystery surrounding her last flight continues to fascinate. A transmission, from 6:15 a.m. to 6:45 a.m. on July 2, 1937, requested radio bearings. She was obviously lost. She was heard, but apparently did not hear the return transmissions from the *U.S. Itasca*, a Navy ship stationed nearby. At 7:42 a.m. her voice was heard saying, "We must be on to you but cannot see you. But gas is running low. Have been unable to reach you by radio. We are flying at 1,000 feet." Her final transmission was received by the *Itasca* at 8:45 a.m: "We are on the line of position 157-337. We are running north and south."

She and Noonan were never heard from again. Although Navy ships scoured the area, no trace of the plane was ever found. Earhart did not carry parachutes, because she felt that they would be little use to her over the Pacific, and they would add too much weight to the aircraft. Neither she nor Noonan knew Morse Code, so they did not carry telegraph equipment on the plane.

Sadly, Howland Island was to be her last stop before she reached Hawaii and familiar territory. She had almost completed her entire trip before she disappeared.

Amelia Earhart's commitment to aviation was both personal and professional and this dedication to aviation remains her legacy today.

Glossary

airspeed indicator: a gauge that measures the speed with which an airplane moves through the air

altimeter: an instrument for measuring height above a given reference level, such as the sea or ground

aviation: the operation of airplanes and other heavier-than-air flying craft, such as helicopters.

Electra: a model of airplane manufactured by Lockheed from 1934 -1941.

flight controls: controls located in the cockpit of the plane, consisting of the yoke and rudder pedals that are used to fly the airplane.

Howland Island: a tiny, uninhabited island in the South Pacific. Amelia Earhart and her plane disappeared en route to Howland Island from Lae, New Guinea.

instrument panel: located in the cockpit of a plane, this section contains the various gauges and guides a pilot needs to determine the speed, direction, and altitude of the craft.

Lockheed: an airplane manufacturing company established in the 1920s. Lockheed is still in business today, manufacturing commercial and private airplanes that are flown throughout the world.

navigator: a person skilled in plotting a course for an aircraft.

runway: a strip of leveled, paved ground for use by airplanes in taking off and landing.

transmission: the passage of radio waves through space between the transmitting station and the receiving station.

Vega: the first model of airplane manufactured by Lockheed in 1927. It became one of the most popular transport planes of the 1920's and early 1930's.

yoke: a lever that operates the tail and wing flaps which guide the plane up and down and side-to-side.

Young Eagles Program: A program of the EAA—Experimental Aircraft Association—in which pilots donate time to take children up in small airplanes. The goal is to excite in children a love of flying and to develop children's interest in aviation.